FRIENDSHIP WITH THE HOLY SPIRIT

THE REVIVAL RELATIONSHIP

John R. Van Gelderen

Friendship With the Holy Spirit:
The Revival Relationship

by John R. Van Gelderen

Printed in the United States of America

ISBN-13: 978-1-60034-862-4
ISBN-10: 1-60034-862-9

Unless otherwise indicated, Bible quotations are taken from the King James Version of the Bible. Personal pronouns of Deity have been capitalized.

www.xulonpress.com

Preach the Word Ministries
P.O. Box 429
Exton, PA 19341
1-800-656-7896
www.ptwm.org

PREFACE

❋

The purpose of this book is to emphasize the relational aspects of the ministry of the Holy Spirit. The focus is purposefully limited to the divine-human relationship. Truly there are many outstanding written works that provide a fuller theology of the Holy Spirit. Also in this work I have not sought to take an academic approach and quote a multitude of authors who take the same position. However, I have provided recommended reading in the back of the book, which emphasizes the same truth which I am emphasizing. My burden is simply to let the authority of the Scripture be the authority. May the Holy Spirit give life to all that is truly founded on the Word of truth.

I would like to give a special thank-you to Sheila Shaw, Sam Keen, Katie Hollandsworth and my wife, Mary Lynn, for typing the manuscript, and Carolyn Cooper for proofing and editing the manuscript.

DEDICATION

To the memory of Charlie Kittrell
a vibrant example of friendship with the Holy Spirit
to the glory of God

TABLE OF CONTENTS

CHAPTER ONE

THE REVIVAL SPIRIT

❊

"We finished at 12:15 A.M. The meeting lasted for nearly two hours in confession, prayer, testimony, and song, again all led by the prompting of the Spirit. The glory of God was being revealed. Dave said he had never been in prayer meetings like these." So reads an entry in my journal from July 2000. Not only had David O'Gorman, my pastor friend in Ireland, never before experienced prayer meetings like these, neither had I. Nor had I ever before known the touch of God like this beyond one service. Yet this was the third consecutive night of glorious two-hour after-meetings (which are simply prayer meetings that are a direct follow-up to the preaching services) finishing around midnight. And more was to come in the next several meetings!

This certainly was a new dimension for me. In fact, I've never been the same. This is true for many others. The lasting impact is remarkable. The Spirit of revival manifested the presence of God so powerfully that backslidden and mediocre saints were restored to spiritual life—life in the Spirit—and the unsaved received eternal life. This was revival! How did it begin?

David O'Gorman says that God had been preparing His people for some time. In various ways God was breaking up fallow ground. To get back to the beginning for me, let me take you to a scene just one week prior to the one I've already described:

> Gray clouds nearly blanketed the sky. A damp, chilly ocean breeze briskly hurried in from the western shoreline approximately one hundred yards away, scampered through the fishing village, and skipped along across the peat bogs to the east. Though the day seemed dreary, my heart thrilled with joy and awesome wonder as I fixed my gaze on the village church in Barvas—a standing reminder of the mighty Spirit of Revival. It was mid-July of 2000. My wife and I were on the Isle of Lewis, located off the northwest coast of Scotland. Just fifty years before this brisk and windy but summer day, the Wind of the Spirit blew across the island. The Lewis Awakening began in December of 1949 in Barvas and continued until 1953 throughout the island. One cannot but think that if God has done it before, and is the unchanging Almighty, He can do it again!
>
> I first became acquainted with the Lewis Revival by reading a brief article about it in the mid-1980s. Immediately my heart was

quickened in reading of God's wonderful works. In the mid-90s, I listened to an audio-tape of Duncan Campbell whom God used as the primary declarer of truth during the revival. Again God stirred my heart deeply. Since then the Lord brought to me several books written by Duncan Campbell, more audiotapes of his preaching, a video of testimonies from the revival, Duncan Campbell's audio and written account of the awakening, and a biography of Campbell. So my wife and I, in God's gracious leading, took a trip to the Isle of Lewis as a part of a missions trip during the summer of 2000. Here God providentially led us to meet and fellowship with four people who were saved during the revival. The glow of God still shines in their countenances. God taught us much in those precious days.

Yet God had been preparing my heart especially in the eight years previous to this trip. After five years as an assistant to my father, Wayne Van Gelderen, Sr., I entered full-time evangelism in January of 1992. At the same time period, my father asked a group of young preachers to read the two-volume biography of Hudson Taylor, written by Taylor's son and daughter-in-law. God used the pen of Hudson Taylor as he exposited certain Bible passages, along with an inductive study of Galatians and Ephesians, to open my eyes to life-changing truths. I saw the futility of flesh-dependence and the absolute necessity of God-dependence to access Spirit-enablement. Those truths budded and blossomed over the next few years. God cultivated faith in my heart during this rich spiritual pilgrimage.

Then on Christmas Day 1998—I'll never forget it—I began reading a Christmas gift from my wife, the book *By My Spirit* by Jonathan Goforth. Though the noise of Christmas festivities surrounded me, I could not put the book down. The printed preaching of Goforth highlighted overlooked promises in the Word of God. God burned in my heart the possibility of an access by faith for revival blessing. Noting that God used an intensive study on the Holy Spirit to bring Goforth to faith regarding revival, I began a similar study.

The impact has been revolutionary. Along the way, God deepened my understanding of God-dependence for Spirit-enabling. "Christ in you" became utterly real and life-changing. Oh, I have failed—but He has never failed when trusted. The Spirit cultivated, and is cultivating, faith for personal and corporate revival.[1]

This study during the first half of 1999 exploded truth across my heart. So in the summer, several of my friends and I met to talk seriously about seeking God's face in revival. We agreed that wherever we were in our various ministries, we would take time to pray daily for the outpouring of the Spirit in revival. Although at times my implementation of this was meager, it was at least a start. Also in my ministry of local church meetings as an evangelist, I began to preach entire series of messages on the ministry of the Holy Spirit.

Another interesting aspect to the story is that in the summer of 1999 my wife Mary Lynn and I discussed what we might do to celebrate our fifteenth wedding anniversary in the summer of 2000. I had been doing a case study of the Lewis Revival and suggested that we go to Scotland to investigate the revival. Mary Lynn was genuinely excited about the idea. So I suggested we pray that God would open a door of ministry in that part of the world. That would help us get over there so that we could also go to Lewis. We began to pray that morning. That evening we received an e-mail from David O'Gorman inviting us back to his church in Ireland for a meeting!

While on Lewis we attended the mid-week service at the church in Barvas where the revival began. Afterwards, the interim pastor, an Irish evangelist who was there for only one month, invited us over to the manse for tea and biscuits. (In America, we would say the parsonage for tea and cookies!)

This evangelist had been trained under Duncan Campbell. His wife's parents were converted during the Lewis Revival. He also invited another pastor and his wife who were there on vacation. Both sets of their parents were converted during the revival. And an older gentleman who himself was converted in the revival was there. What blessed fellowship we had!

We talked much of revival. At times, we would stop and sing a hymn. Often, they would sing a Psalm. (I wish we could learn to do that in America!) We also prayed together. Truly, it was a blessed time. In fact, later the older gentleman wrote me a letter and said that the time at the manse reminded him of times during the revival!

On the way back across the island, Mary Lynn noted that these individuals had been following the Holy Spirit. There was nothing manipulated in what they did. It was a spontaneous following of the Spirit. The thought impressed me greatly.

Several days later, we were in Dublin, Ireland. I preached in the Sunday morning service. Afterwards, we fellowshipped with our good friends David and Valerie O'Gorman over dinner. I told them much of what I've rehearsed in the previous paragraphs. At the end, Valerie wondered out loud where God might take all of this.

The next day, the church met at a camp in Avoca, Ireland. That week I preached a series on the ministry of the Holy Spirit, dealing with the Spirit-filled life which is the very essence of the revived life. Monday ended with a "singspiration." However, I did not sense the life of God in it. This would not help the church camp. I prayed that if God wanted me to speak with David about it, that He would open the way to do so. The following morning God answered my prayer as I came across my pastor friend while I was out on a walk.

When I mentioned that I did not sense the life of God in the singspiration, he agreed. In reminding him of our time in Lewis, I suggested that we depend on the Holy Spirit to guide our time. So, after preaching in the morning and then again in the evening—and God's breath was on that service as I preached on Galatians 2:20—David announced that we would meet again after the dessert time, but that we were going to do things a little differently. He said he would explain at the meeting.

At about 10:00 P.M., I suppose about thirty or so folks came. We were seated in a circle of chairs. David said something to the effect of, "We're going to do things a little differently tonight. I am turning this meeting over to the Holy Spirit. I know it may sound a little scary. But let's just depend on the Spirit. If He leads you to sing, start singing and we'll join in. If He leads you to pray, pray. If He leads you to testify, then give a testimony. But don't do anything unless the Spirit leads you to do so. Let's depend on Him."

Since the previous night was a typical singspiration, you might expect there to be singing. But instead someone began to pray; after he finished, then another. Within about ten minutes I was aware that God was meeting with His people! There was nothing weird. It was just an awareness of the presence of God. This, of course, makes one aware of his sin. Soon people were confessing their sins. Amazingly, neither Dave nor I had mentioned confession—not that it would have been improper to do so, but we hadn't. Oh, what brokenness before the Lord! Nothing inappropriate was said, but there was a proper transparency before God and men. The meeting lasted for two hours and seemed like fifteen minutes. I suppose the first third of the meeting was primarily praying. The middle third broke out into glorious singing as people now had come clean with God. Oh, the joy of a cleansed conscience and clean heart! The last third of the meeting went back to praying. This time it was an intense praying for God to spread His work and save the lost.

I should mention there were two unsaved people in that meeting who got saved that night. One was a young, outgoing girl who said to her parents afterwards, "I'm afraid. These people know God and I don't." The other was a deaf teenage boy who, although he couldn't hear the prayers, sensed the presence of God. He nudged someone next to him. When they went out, he communicated that he felt as if his chest was going to burst and he wanted to get saved!

God met with us night after night. It was the first time I had experienced a sustained moving of God on this fashion beyond just one night. Many were changed. The impact has continued. Young people who were once worldly have attended Bible college to prepare for the ministry. The church has grown and seen far more people saved since then than ever before.

In Ireland I saw demonstrated in a deeper way the living reality of dependence on the Spirit—and the blessed effects. Of course, this was a corporate setting. Yet the individual impact on me and many others has been forever life changing, because the same dynamic transforms individual lives.

A classic testimony of personal revival comes from the life of Walter Wilson. He relates the following in his book on the Holy Spirit entitled *Ye Know Him*:

> The first seventeen years of my life, after meeting the Saviour were years of much Bible study, much activity, and no fruit. I had been taught that it was wrong to expect any fruit. Teachers had also instructed me to not speak to the Holy Spirit in prayer nor commune with Him about the work of God but to go to the Father with every matter. The barrenness of my ministry and the lack of results in my service was the cause of no little sorrow and regret.
>
> One day the Lord graciously sent across my path a man of God who said to me, "What is the Holy Spirit to you?" I replied that He was one of the persons of the Godhead. The servant of God answered that this was a true statement but did not answer his question, "What is the Holy Spirit *to* you? What does He mean *to* you?" This inquiry produced a deep heart searching and I replied, "He is nothing to me at all. I know who He is, but I have no personal relationship with Him." My friend assured me that my life was barren and my ministry fruitless because of this neglect. I had been treating the Holy Spirit as a servant of mine. I would ask Him to come help me when I would teach a class. To be more explicit, I really asked the Father to send His Spirit to help me. This left the Spirit as a

servant subject to my call and request. He was never more than an agent of the Godhead to serve me whenever I felt His need and asked the Father for His ministry.

The message which this Christian brought to my heart roused within me a great desire to know the Spirit and to serve Him successfully. I had a fear, however, of doing the wrong thing and felt that perhaps the Father and Lord Jesus would be offended if I should go directly to the Spirit about any matter. About this time . . .[2]

We will finish this story later. What about you? What is the Holy Spirit *to you*? What does He mean *to you?* In other words, how is your relationship with the Holy Spirit? Is there a vibrant genuine relationship? Would you say you have a friendship with the Holy Spirit?

Our opening Scripture text for this study is the benediction found in II Corinthians 13:14: "The grace of the Lord Jesus Christ, and the love of God, and the communion of the Holy Ghost, be with you all. Amen." Our focus will be the phrase *the communion of the Holy Spirit.* Notice the inspired prayer of the Apostle reveals a burden for *all* to know this *communion.* This by way of application includes every believer today.

The keyword of our text, *communion,* means "partnership, fellowship, sharing together, companionship, joint participation, or functioning together as one." What a picturesque term! What a friendship!

Since we are to commune with the Holy Spirit, we must develop a friendship with our Heavenly Partner. Yet how can the believer as the human partner develop a biblically balanced, vibrant relationship with the Spirit as the Heavenly Partner? Foundationally, in order to fulfill our responsibility in this miraculous friendship, we must understand who our Heavenly Partner really is *to us*. This will provide insight into our relational responsibilities to Him. So from the vast realm of scriptural truth regarding the Holy Spirit, let's focus on four biblical affirmations of who He is to us. This topical exposition will guide us through the next four chapters, and then we'll begin to draw some conclusions in the final chapters.

Endnotes

1. John R. Van Gelderen, *The Wind of the Spirit in Personal and Corporate Revival* (Menomonee Falls, Wis.: Preach the Word Ministries, Inc., 2003), pp. 1–2.

2. Walter Wilson, *Ye Know Him* (Grand Rapids: Zondervan, 1939), pp. 10–11.

CHAPTER TWO

THE DIVINE PARTNER

❦

One of the stirring chapters of revival history is the Korean Revival of 1907. In Jonathan Goforth's account of this mighty revival, he emphasizes that the Korean saints honored the Holy Spirit. When they began to honor the Spirit, they stopped quenching the Spirit of revival and revival fires swept Korea. According to Rosalind Goforth, Jonathan's sermon "When the Spirit's Fire Swept Korea" (which preaches the story) was his most blessed message.[1]

Our text in II Corinthians 13:14 delineates the Godhead by referring to "the grace of the Lord Jesus Christ, and the love of God [the Father], and the communion of the Holy Ghost." Since the Holy Spirit is the Divine Partner, we must honor the Spirit as God. Let's ask some questions to guide us through this chapter.

Is the Holy Spirit Truly God?
This question seems almost unnecessary. Undoubtedly, many would answer yes. Yet for many,

saying that the Holy Spirit is God is merely a doctrinal affirmation rather than a practical reality. The Holy Spirit is not really given the status of Deity by many in the practice of their daily lives. Therefore, practically they are not true Trinitarians, because although they acknowledge the Spirit as God in their doctrine, they do not treat Him as God in their practice.

However, in Matthew 28:19 Jesus commands us to make disciples and baptize them in the name [singular] of the Father, and of the Son, and of the Holy Spirit. The Spirit is thus given the status of the Godhead. He is omnipresent in Psalm 139. Only God is omnipresent. He is called "the eternal Spirit" in Hebrews 9:14. Only God is eternal. The Spirit is Deity; He is God.

Should the Holy Spirit Be Glorified as God?

A preacher once came to me quite exercised and exclaimed, "You can't glorify the Spirit!" But where does it say that in the Bible? If you cannot glorify the Spirit, He is less than God, and you no longer have a true Trinity. Others object saying, "You're placing too much emphasis on the Holy Spirit." But how can you place too much emphasis on God? This reveals the real problem—that for some the Holy Spirit is less than God. Would anyone say "You're placing too much emphasis on the Father" or "You're placing too much emphasis on Jesus Christ?" Why does the Holy Spirit not receive the honor due to One who is a part of the Godhead? Now if one were to uplift one person of the Godhead to the total exclusion of the other two, that would be false doctrine. But that is not the issue here. This is not a matter of de-empha-sizing the Father or the Son; it is a matter of recog-nizing that you must not neglect the Holy Spirit. This is not a matter of getting out of balance; it is a matter of getting back into balance.

Some object, citing John 16:14 when Jesus, referring to the Spirit, said, "He shall glorify Me." While this is most certainly true, Jesus never said that we are not to honor the Spirit. Some take a leap at this point that jumps beyond what Jesus actually said. They conclude you *cannot* glorify the Spirit. Scripturally, there is a sense where each person of the Godhead glorifies the other two. As A.W. Tozer points out, the persons of the Godhead are not jealous of each other!

Others object, citing John 16:13 where Jesus said of the Spirit, "He shall not speak of Himself." They argue from this that we are not to speak about or talk about the Holy Spirit. Amazingly, this verse is in a three-chapter-long sermon about the Holy Spirit preached by Christ Himself! Notice as well that Jesus did not say, "He shall not speak *about* Himself," but *"of* Himself." The term translated *of* literally means "from." The Spirit does not speak *from* Himself apart from the Father and the Son. The Godhead always works in perfect unison. The truth is the Holy Spirit does speak *about* Himself. How else could we know about the Spirit except through the inspired Word that "came not in old time by the will of man: but holy men of God spake as they were moved by the Holy Ghost" (II Peter 1:21)? The Scripture contains 347 explicit references to the Holy Spirit: 86 in the Old

Testament and 261 in the New Testament. In light of the relative brevity of the New Testament, is this not a considerable number? Yet this does not include words like *grace* in which the Spirit is implicitly mentioned. This in no way diminishes the greater number of references to Christ in keeping with the Spirit's role to "testify of Me [the Son]" (John 15:26). But it does show that it is legitimate to talk about the Holy Spirit.

Also, if you interpret the phrase *He shall not speak of Himself* to mean "*about* Himself," then in order to be consistent you would have to interpret the phrase in John 14:10, where Jesus said "I speak not of Myself," the same way. If the former phrase means we are not to talk about the Spirit, then the latter phrase would mean we are not to speak about Christ. This of course would be folly!

II Corinthians 3:17 states, "Now the Lord is that Spirit." Inspiration teaches the Lordship of the Spirit. The Holy Spirit is coequal with the Father and the Son and may rightly be glorified as such. Since He is Lord, He should be honored as Lord! The Nicene Creed written over 1600 years ago says, "I believe in the Holy Ghost, the Lord and Giver of life, which proceedeth from the Father and the Son, and with the Father and the Son together is worshipped and glorified." The Athanasian Creed written over 1500 years ago states, "Such as the Father is, such is the Son, and such is the Holy Ghost." Remember the oneness of God. Although there are three persons in the Godhead, there is only one God. Therefore in honoring God, we may rightly honor each person of the Godhead. The "Doxology" articulates the truth so well:

> Praise God, from whom all blessings flow;
> Praise Him, all creatures here below;
> Praise Him above, ye heav'nly host;
> Praise Father, Son, and Holy Ghost!

Who Reveals Christ?

Who revealed the Father? The Son, for Jesus said in John 14:9, "He that hath seen Me hath seen the Father." Who then reveals the Son? The Spirit, for Jesus said in John 16:14, "He shall glorify Me: for He shall receive of Mine, and shall show it unto you." Notice the Spirit shows us Christ. He reveals the Son. As the Son reveals the Father, so the Spirit reveals the Son. Why is this important?

Jesus said in John 5:23, "That all men should honour the Son, even as they honour the Father." Why? Because the Son is the express revelation of the Father. Then Jesus continued saying, "He that honoureth not the Son honoureth not the Father which hath sent Him." Why? Since the Son reveals the Father, if you do not honor the Son, you cannot be truly honoring the Father. Therefore, for example, when the Jehovah's Witnesses claim to honor the Father yet deny the deity of Christ, they are deceived. Since the Son reveals the Father, in order to honor the Father, you must honor the Son.

In light of this principle, if you desire to honor the Son, whom must you honor? The Spirit, for the Spirit reveals the Son who sent Him. Do you see the point? The Spirit is our only access to seeing Jesus!

The Spirit shows us Christ (John 16:14). If you do not honor the Spirit and thus rightly relate to the Spirit, then you block your avenue of seeing Jesus. So if you have a passion for the Lord Jesus Christ, if you desire that Christ be exalted in your sight, if you long to know Him and the power of His resurrection, then you must properly relate to the Holy Spirit, for the Spirit is the One who will glorify Christ and reveal Christ to you.

Near the end of a week-long meeting at which I preached on the ministry of the Holy Spirit, members of a local church sang "Victory in Jesus." The pastor later commented to me that his people were singing that song on a new level. He noted that although the preaching dealt with the truths of the Spirit, the effect was the exaltation of Christ! And should we be surprised?

What Is the Spirit Like?

The Spirit is like Jesus, for Philippians 1:19 calls Him "the Spirit of Jesus Christ." When Philip requested of Jesus, "Lord, show us the Father, and it sufficeth [is sufficient for] us," Jesus responded with that heart-searching question, "Have I been so long time with you, and yet hast thou not known Me?" Then He declared, "He that hath seen Me hath seen the Father" (John 14:8–9). So perhaps the Spirit responds to us in similar tones, "Have I been so long time with you, and yet hast thou not known Me? He that hath known Me hath known the Son."

In John 12:44–45, Jesus said, "He that believeth on Me, believeth not on Me, but on Him that sent Me.

And he that seeth Me seeth Him that sent Me." The principle shown here implies that he who believes in the Holy Spirit believes not in the Holy Spirit, but in Christ who sent Him. And he who sees (spiritually) the Holy Spirit sees (spiritually) Christ who sent Him. This is how we see Jesus today! In fact, in John 14:16–18 Jesus said to His disciples that He was sending the Spirit. Although the world does not know the Spirit, Jesus emphasized to His disciples "ye know Him; for He dwelleth with you, and shall be in you." Then Jesus re-states the same truth in a different way: "I will not leave you comfortless: **I** will come to you." Therefore, it is not just a matter of the Spirit coming in Christ's stead, but the Spirit bringing Christ to you! If you long to know Christ intimately, you must get to know the Spirit. As you do, you will surely exclaim, "What a friend we have in Jesus!"

On a personal note, there was a time in my life when although I was saved I did not sense a close relationship with the Lord Jesus. This bothered me and at the same time puzzled me. However, since the Lord has stirred me to develop a right relationship with the Holy Spirit, the Son has risen gloriously in my view! Now seeing Jesus is everything! The more we relate to the Spirit of Jesus, the more the Son of Righteousness rises in our view and will rise until we see Him in His full-orbed glory!

When the Third Great Awakening commenced in America, Spurgeon preached to his people the following:

It is the work of the Holy Spirit that I wish to especially direct to your attention, and may I as well mention the reason why I do. It is this: in the United States of America there has been a great awakening [1858]. Two hundred and fifty thousand people profess to have been regenerated. . . . Now this great work in America has been manifestly caused by the outpouring of the Spirit. . . . To have a similar effect produced in this land, the one thing we must seek is the outpouring of the Holy Spirit. I thought that perhaps my writing about the work of the Holy Spirit might fulfill the text, "Them that honor me I will honor" (I Samuel 2:30). My sincere desire is to honor the Holy Spirit, and if He will be pleased to honor His church in return, unto Him be the glory forever.[2]

The Third Great Awakening did spread across the sea to England and beyond! Since the Holy Spirit is the Divine Partner, you must honor the Spirit as God. This must be true not only in doctrine, but in practice. May the Spirit then be pleased by granting His reviving presence.

Endnotes

1. Jonathan Goforth, *When the Spirit's Fire Swept Korea* (Elkhart, Ind.: Bethel Publishing, 1984).

2. C. H. Spurgeon, *Power for You* (New Kensington, Pa.: Whitaker House, reprint 1996), pp. 10–11.

CHAPTER THREE

A PERSONAL PARTNER

❊

On the other end of the phone line, I heard an excited voice exclaim, "John, I just wanted to let you know what God did!" It was Sunday. A pastor friend from my previous meeting the week before was calling. I had just preached in his church on the ministry of the Holy Spirit. Though he did not have a resisting spirit, he admitted to grappling with what he was hearing (especially the truth which this chapter presents). Yet on that Sunday in his church, he preached from Acts 1–2. At the conclusion, he confessed to neglecting the Holy Spirit. He told his people that he was going to be the first to kneel in prayer at the conclusion of the service. Then he offered for others to whom God had spoken to join him. Although while I was there the week before, public response was minimal, yet about thirty people joined him! In the months following, the church saw remarkable blessings and movements of God.

Our text in II Corinthians 13:14 says *the communion of the Holy Ghost, be with you all.* We noted earlier that the word *communion* [*koinonia*] means "partnership, fellowship, sharing together, companionship, joint participation, functioning together as one." It is a beautiful term of friendship. Also the definite article *the* before the name *Holy Spirit* grammatically emphasizes His person. Since the Holy Spirit is a Personal Partner, we must fellowship with the Spirit as a person. Let's consider two key thoughts.

The Holy Spirit Is a Personality

The Spirit of God is not an inanimate object. Yet how often do people look for some kind of spiritual signpost to point the way? But the Spirit is not a signpost or a commodity; He is a person.

The Spirit of God is not an impersonal force. Yet how often do Christians say, "Something told me..." But the Spirit is not a something; He is Someone. Sadly, for many He is nothing more than an impersonal force. Often this is evidenced when people refer to the Spirit as "it." How would you like to be referred to as an "it"?

Throughout the Upper Room Discourse in John 14–16, the Lord Jesus refers to the Holy Spirit repeatedly as "Him" and "He." Do you get the biblical picture? *He*, not *it*, brooded over the face of the waters in Genesis 1. *He*, not *it*, strove with man in Genesis 6, and so forth throughout the Scriptures. The point is that if you are truly born of the Spirit, then *He*, not *it*, lives in you! He is your personal partner. The Spirit-filled life accesses a Life—a Person—who lives in you to live through you.

The Spirit loves, and therefore can be grieved. Ephesians 4:30 says, "And grieve not the Holy Spirit of God, whereby ye are sealed unto the day of redemption." Mere forces, ideas, or influences cannot love and be grieved. The Spirit stirs the heart, and therefore can be quenched. I Thessalonians 5:19 says, "Quench not the Spirit." The Spirit teaches, convinces, and leads, and therefore can be resisted. Acts 7:51 says, "Ye do always resist the Holy Ghost."

Do you treat the Holy Spirit as a person? Personality must be cultivated. You may be introduced to someone, and therefore you know their name. But do you really know them? Obviously, it takes interaction to cultivate their personality. Even so, everyone who is born of the Spirit has been introduced to the Spirit. But it takes interaction to cultivate personality. It takes fellowshipping to cultivate friendship. This leads us to our second key thought.

A Friendship Is a Relationship

What makes a good relationship? Communication, appreciation, devotion, and loyalty quickly come to mind. Are not these relational concepts crucial to relating? Again I refer to our text. *Communion* means "fellowship, sharing together, and joint participation." In fact, the same word is translated in Philippians 2:1 as "fellowship" in the phrase *fellowship of the Spirit*. The very term demands an interactive relationship. *Communion* must be mutual or it is not communion.

Open Communication

Foundational to any healthy relationship is open communication. Since this is the case and yet the most confused point in people's minds, we will spend the majority of our time on this truth. Romans 8:16 says, "The Spirit [Himself] beareth witness with our spirit." Notice where He bears witness: *with our spirit*. He speaks to our inner man, not our outer man. Understanding this can help protect against counterfeits. But He does communicate to individual believers. Is this communication to be only a one-way communication? Sadly for many this is the case, and therefore they do not treat the Holy Spirit as a person. They may acknowledge intellectually the personhood of the Spirit, but in practice they really do not depend on this reality. They overlook the practical ramifications of "the Holy Ghost which is in you" (I Corinthians 6:19).

Walter Wilson states the matter with so much common sense: "Personal presence automatically carries with it privileges of conversation." You do not have to get permission to talk to a person! If you cannot communicate with the Holy Spirit, then what is the Holy Spirit to you but a mere force, or a mysterious power, or an inanimate object?

What kind of marriage would a couple have if only one partner did all the talking? (We won't go where we could go with this!) This kind of marriage partnership would be unhealthy and weak. To have a good relationship, each partner must relate. Two-way communication is necessary for a strong, healthy relationship.

Yet does the Bible teach us to communicate with the Holy Spirit? The answer is yes—both explicitly and implicitly. On the explicit level our text, II Corinthians 13:14, an inspired benediction, says, *the communion of the Holy Ghost, be with you all.* Clearly it is God's will for each believer to commune with the Spirit. To commune, to fellowship, to share together, and to function together as one in joint participation inherently demands two-way communication. Communication must be mutual or it is not communion. If words have meaning and language has integrity, in order for *the communion of the Holy Spirit* to *be with* us as individuals, we must join in this relationship of God with men. Isn't it absolutely amazing that God desires companionship with us? What a great salvation!

On the implicit level, in the longest treatise on the Holy Spirit given by Christ Himself in John 14–16, Christ says, "And I will pray the Father, and He shall give you another Comforter." The term *another* means "another of the same kind." Then Jesus says in the next verse, "I will not leave you comfortless [lit., as orphans]: I will come to you." The Spirit brings Christ to you. To despise or slight the Spirit is to despise or slight "Christ in you!"

Another of the same kind has come to stand in Christ's stead and yet to bring Christ to you. Did not the disciples interact with Jesus as a person? Did they not communicate with Him? Since the Spirit is another of the same kind, should we not interact with the Spirit today as the disciples of old did with Christ?

The issue is communication, not necessarily praying. In a marriage relationship when a husband and wife communicate with each other, they are not praying to each other (unless the wife is asking for the wallet!). The issue is interaction through communication.

However, is it improper to ever address the Holy Spirit in prayer? Is it improper to trust Him as God? The answers ought to be obvious. Yet many get hung up here, and in the name of honoring Jesus or the Father, they dishonor the Spirit of Jesus and the Spirit of the Father. Is this not a contradiction? Let's take just a moment to clear up some of the confusion.

I suppose the greatest objection to ever directly addressing the Spirit comes from a misunderstanding of "The Lord's Prayer." The Lord Jesus said in Matthew 6:9, "After this manner therefore pray ye: Our Father . . ." So some conclude from this that we are to address only the Father, but this conclusion is problematic in several ways. First, if this means you can address only the Father, then to be consistent you could not ever address the Son. Do not many people get saved by asking Jesus to save them? Second, if we are to take from this that you can only say *Our Father,* then to be consistent you could only pray the exact words of The Lord's Prayer whenever you prayed. This of course would be the vain repetitions of the Roman Catholic "Our Fathers." Third, to take from this that you can only say *Our Father* is to miss Christ's opening concept of "After this manner therefore pray ye." The issue here is *manner*, not vain repetition.

The fact is many people at the time of Christ did pray to Jesus (not the Father) to have mercy on them. Peter as he began to sink prayed, "Lord, save me." Should not we, who live in the age of the Spirit, at appropriate times cry out to the Spirit as our Helper in time of need? Some object, saying that with Christ, He was personally standing there with them. But is that not the whole point? The Holy Spirit is just as personally present, not only with us, but in us! To not apprehend this truth is to miss the blessing of the indwelling Christ.

The Book of Acts records thirteen prayers. Twelve are addressed to "Lord," not "Our Father." Some contexts infer Christ, and in one instance Christ is named. The truth is *Lord* encompasses all three persons of the Godhead or can be used specifically with any one person, including the Holy Spirit. II Corinthians 3:17 states, "Now the Lord is that Spirit." In II Thessalonians 3:5, Paul under inspiration said, "And the Lord direct your hearts into the love of God, and into the patient waiting for Christ." The implication is "And may the Lord . . . ," which is essentially a prayer. Also since the Father and the Son are named in the last two phrases, the implication is that *the Lord* in the first phrase (to whom Paul prayed) refers to the Spirit. Quite frankly, as you go throughout the day and cry out "Lord, give me wisdom," who are you talking to?

In this specific sense, Jesus said in Matthew 9:38, "Pray ye therefore the Lord of the harvest, that

He will send forth laborers into His harvest." Who
is *the Lord of the harvest*? The context definitely
leans toward the idea that Christ is here referring to
someone else other than His specific person. Who
descended in mighty power on the day of Pentecost
so that 3,000 people were harvested? We are explicitly told this was the Spirit (Acts 2). Who told Philip
in Acts 8 to "Go near, and join thyself to this chariot"
so that the Ethiopian eunuch was harvested? We are
explicitly told this was the Spirit (Acts 8:29). Who
said to Peter in Acts 10, "Go with them, doubting
nothing" so that Cornelius and his household were
harvested, thus opening the way to the Gentile
harvest? We are explicitly told this was the Spirit
(Acts 10:19–20). Who said to the church at Antioch
in Acts 13, "Separate Me Barnabas and Saul for the
work whereunto I have called them," which was the
first missionary journey of multiple harvests? We
are explicitly told this was the Spirit (Acts 13:2).
Who forbade Paul in Acts 16 to minister in Asia and
Bithynia in order to get them into the Macedonian
harvest? We are explicitly told this was the Spirit
(Acts 16:6–7). So who is *the Lord of the harvest*?
The Book of Acts certainly implies this is the Holy
Spirit. And Jesus said, "**Pray** ye therefore the Lord
of the harvest, that He will send forth laborers into
His harvest."

Do not the hymn writers of the past reflect a
proper understanding of appropriate times to address
the Spirit in prayer? For example "Spirit of God,
Descend upon My Heart;" "Breathe on Me Breath
of God;" "Spirit of the Living God, Fall Fresh on

Me;" and "Holy Ghost, with Light Divine." Charles Wesley wrote "Come, Holy Ghost, our Hearts Inspire," "Come, Thou Everlasting Spirit," and "Spirit of Faith, Come Down." Isaac Watts wrote, "Eternal Spirit! Praise We Bring." All of these examples directly address the Holy Spirit in prayer. Were all these hymn writers misled? Are congregations sinning every time they sing one of these prayers? Obviously former generations had a better understanding of this issue than the present generation.

This is not at all to diminish the Father. He is *Our Father*, and much of the time we most certainly will beseech Him as such. In fact the Spirit enables us to do so. Romans 8:15 says, "But ye have received the Spirit of adoption, whereby we cry, Abba, Father." Also this in no way should imply a minimizing of the Son. Oh, "that in all things He might have the pre-eminence!" That is the whole point. This is to say that where applicable we must stop slighting the blessed Holy Spirit, who is both the Spirit of the Father and the Spirit of the Son. This is not a matter of getting out of balance, but rather of getting back into balance.

Once while in Ireland, a man asked, "Can we just say 'Lord' and let God address it to the appropriate Person?" I love the simplicity of this question. There is a sense in which addressing any one person of the Godhead is addressing all three since you are dealing with one God. The problem comes when people willfully neglect the Holy Spirit.

All three persons of the Godhead are often mentioned regarding a specific matter in Scripture, but One is emphasized as the prominent One in that particular matter. This both reveals the oneness of God, and yet the distinctiveness of each person. When the Spirit is emphasized regarding a matter, then we may properly address Him about that matter. The Holy Spirit is the Comforter. How can He truly be the Comforter if we cannot bare to Him our tale of woe? As the *Paraclete,* He is the Helper. Should we not cry out for help in time of need? He is the Lord of the harvest. Should we not talk to Him about guidance and enablement regarding our partnership with Him in the harvest? He is the great Teacher. Should we not ask the author of the inspired Word for illumination of the sacred page? This is the cry of the psalmist in Psalm 119:18: "Open thou mine eyes, that I may behold wondrous things out of Thy law." When the Spirit is the direct Agent involved, then He may be addressed just as our praying would be addressed to the Father or the Son, depending on the purpose of the communication.

Again, however, the real issue is not prayer as such, but rather communication. The Holy Spirit is a person and must be treated as a person. Suppose you are visiting a museum which specializes in ancient artifacts. Suppose three others are making the visit with you, but one of them is appointed as your personal guide. Would it be right to only speak to the other two and never to the one who is in regular communication with you? Yet is this not what many do to the Spirit?

Jesus said in John 16:7, "It is expedient for you [it is to your advantage] that I go away: for if I go not away, the Comforter will not come unto you: but if I depart, I will send Him unto you." What a statement! Jesus said it is more advantageous for us if He departs so that His Spirit would come and be our personal companion. To ignore this personal relationship with the Spirit is to despise our Savior's throne gift that He sent on the Day of Pentecost.

An evangelist friend of mine years ago heard Walter Wilson preach. Wilson began by asking the audience how many of them had spoken to the Holy Spirit that day. There was little response. Then he said that since the Holy Spirit is a person who lives in you, He is always with you; and to have a person always with you and yet never speak to Him is not very nice! This little anecdote certainly helps put the issue into perspective. As John R. Rice once said, "When you know the family, you can speak to all the family members!"

Now I recognize, especially in light of the overreaction of our day to strange fire, that many may have never thought much about interaction with the Holy Spirit and are not willfully neglecting Him. This is one matter. It is entirely another matter to willfully neglect interacting with the Holy Spirit as a person. When this is the case, it reveals on the part of the one involved a lack of honoring the Spirit as truly God and a lack of treating the Spirit as truly a person. This reveals a lack of understanding of the genuine Spirit-filled life of Galatians 2:20: "I live; yet not I, but Christ liveth in me." This keeps God's people from accessing the victory of Christ for holiness and service.

Expressed Appreciation

When someone does something for you, courtesy demands you say "thank you." How often do we ignore the Spirit on this score? While we may rightly thank the Father and the Son, do we forget to thank the Spirit? When our relationship with the Spirit is healthy, gratitude will flow to the Spirit for all His guidance, comfort, and aid. After discovering some arresting truth in Scripture, how often do we say, "I found a wonderful truth today!" Is this not arrogantly slighting the Spirit? Is not the reality that the Spirit of truth guided us into truth? When the partnership is properly developed, we can say as the early Christians did in Acts 15:28, "For it seemed good to the Holy Ghost, and to us." This inspired example expresses appreciation.

Loyal Devotion

Another key to developing a good relationship is loyal devotion. The Spirit is certainly a loyal and devoted partner. As the Spirit of Christ, He never leaves us, nor forsakes us (Hebrews 13:5–6). The next chapter will unfold our responsibility of loyal devotion to our Heavenly Partner.

Since the Holy Spirit is a Personal Partner, we must fellowship with Him as a person. One lady, after apprehending this truth, said, "It was so good to talk with the Holy Spirit!" This makes our walk with God personal and real. Just as salvation is not a religion, but a relationship with Jesus Christ, so the Spirit-filled life is not a religion, but a relationship with the Holy Spirit.

I remember well when revival swept through a small group of praying believers in the Philippines. We were in the midst of a conference on the Spirit-filled life. As the Spirit of judgment came in power among us, sin was earnestly confessed. Soon, wearied believers exchanged spiritual dullness for spiritual joy. As a result of clean hearts and filled lives, God gave a harvest of souls over the next weeks and months which that generation had not seen before in their church. If God has spoken to you about neglecting the Holy Spirit, may your response be as one Filipino pastor prayed, "O Holy Spirit, forgive me for not treating You as a person!"

CHAPTER FOUR

THE SENIOR PARTNER

❦

Y ears ago, James A. Stewart, an evangelist from Scotland, was preaching in the Orkney Islands. Feeling impressed of the Lord to do so, he got alone with God by walking a cold beach in the early morning hours. He knew God had brought him out there for a purpose. There he became convinced of the Spirit to go to Riga in Latvia. He closed the meetings, and within days arrived unannounced and unknown in the eastern European city of Riga. When a certain pastor invited him to preach, God sent revival blessing! For months Stewart preached throughout many eastern European countries. Saints were revived, and literally thousands were saved as God poured out His Spirit.[1] Truly, he was in partnership with the Spirit and knew it. He knew the Spirit's voice. He discerned the difference between the counterfeit guidance of impulse and the sure convincement of the Spirit. This and other similar accounts are given in both his autobiography *I Must Tell* and his biography *James Stewart:*

Missionary.[2] Oh, how we need to learn to recognize and obey the Senior Partner!

Our text in II Corinthians 13:14 says *the communion of the Holy Ghost, be with you all*. Clearly the Holy Spirit as the Heavenly Partner is the Senior Partner. Since the Holy Spirit is the Senior Partner, you must yield to the Spirit as Lord.

As we have noted in previous chapters, II Corinthians 3:17 says, "Now the Lord is that Spirit." The Spirit is called *Lord*. The Spirit is Lord because the Holy Spirit is the Spirit of Christ and Christ is the head of the church. When Paul prayed in II Thessalonians 3:5, "And the Lord direct your hearts into the love of God, and into the patient waiting for Christ," he calls the Spirit *Lord*. The Lordship of Christ is executed through the Lordship of the Spirit.

Since the Spirit is Lord, you must surrender to His lordship. You must yield your will to the will of Another. This is not passivity. Passivity would be giving up your will, and stopping short at that. However that is the devil's playground. Surrender to the Spirit is giving up your will, and taking on His will. It is exchanging your will for the Spirit's will. This is you making a choice to embrace the Spirit's will instead of your own will. This is not the Spirit instead of you, but you cooperating with the Spirit. This is not idle passivity, but active cooperation. This is true surrender.

II Corinthians 3:17 says, "Now the Lord is that Spirit: and where the Spirit of the Lord is, there is liberty." You must not only recognize that the Spirit is Lord, but also yield to Him as Lord. The second phrase implies "where the Spirit is Lord" or more clearly "where the Spirit is yielded to as Lord." This implies dependence on the Spirit's leadership. Your will must be brought into union with the Spirit's will. Where does this begin?

Directional Surrender

Partnership with the Holy Spirit begins with a directional surrender. Romans 12:1 urges "I beseech you therefore, brethren . . . that ye present your bodies . . . unto God." Which person of the Godhead indwells the believer? The Spirit. Now why does Romans 12:1 urge believers to present their bodies to the Spirit of God when I Corinthians 6:19 states, "your body is the temple of Holy Ghost which is in you"? Because when you got saved, the Spirit specifically moved into your spirit. Romans 12:1 presents the body to the Spirit so that He who dwells in your spirit may possess all of you.

How many of you would bring a guest into your home and show him into the guest room only to lock him in? If you are saved, the Spirit indwells your spirit, your innermost chamber. What do you do if He steps into the kitchen of your appetites? How do you respond when He opens the closet of your hidden sins? If we deny Him access to any chamber of our lives, we are not giving Him full control of our lives. Remember, He can be quenched. Is it not amazing that although He is the Almighty God, the Spirit as the Heavenly Dove does not force Himself on the human will? On the other hand, He is Lord whether or not you recognize Him as such; but in order for you to fully benefit from His lordship, you must recognize Him as Lord.

It is possible to purchase a product, possess the title deed, and yet not have the product delivered to you for hands-on possession until a later time. Likewise, when you trusted Christ as Savior, Jesus, who purchased you with His own blood, took the title deed of your life in hand. Romans 12:1 is simply delivering to the Spirit of Jesus what He already owns for full hands-on possession. Since Christ owns you, unsurrender is really a theft against Deity. Surrender is not just an honorable act on your part; it is a responsible duty.

For James A. Stewart, like the Apostle Paul, this surrender came nearly simultaneously with his salvation. But for many this surrender often comes later when they not only have come to the end of themselves for salvation, but also for sanctification. Usually there is a point of surrender where they have, in essence, been saying no to God. For example, when F. B. Meyer was confronted with absolute surrender, he admitted his soul recoiled at the thought. This revealed his lack of surrender beneath the surface. Having supposedly given all to God, he was yet hanging on to one key to one room in his life. Although not finding himself willing, when he finally cried out, "Lord, I'm willing for you to make me willing," he was quickly enabled to give up the issue. That is surrender—giving up! But in his yielding, great blessing followed and F. B. Meyer still impacts many today through his God-blessed writings.

Often surrender crystallizes down to a point of surrender. It is the point where a believer, in essence, says "no" to the Spirit. Many times this is not an obvious issue, but rather among the "doubtful things" that truly test surrender. During a meeting a pastor told me on a Monday night that on Sunday night (the previous night), he sensed the Spirit wanted him to give up a particular television program that he and his wife watched regularly on Sunday nights to relax after the Sunday evening service. As the Spirit brought conviction, this became a point of surrender. So on that Sunday night, he and his wife gave it up. He explained with joy that he was sensitive to the Holy Spirit's reality all day Monday. Surrender "sensitized" him. By the end of the meeting, this pastor had truly experienced personal revival. He cringed as he commented, "I wonder what I would have missed if I had not obeyed the Spirit's leading on Sunday night!"

The point of surrender may differ for you. If it is an ambition that is not God's will for you, give it up. If the Spirit puts His finger on an issue of worldliness in your life that you are savoring—perhaps a certain CD, or DVD, or article of clothing— give it up. If there is a spiritually unhealthy relationship in your life, give it up. Surrender to the Spirit, and take His will for you.

This presentation of *all* to the Spirit is the initial entrance into the Spirit-filled life. But partnership is ongoing and demands continual surrender. The presentation is a directional surrender, but the practice is a daily surrender. It is the "living sacrifice."

Daily Surrender

Partnership with the Holy Spirit continues with a daily surrender. Ephesians 5:18 commands, "Be filled with the Spirit." The grammatical idea here is a continual yielding to the leadership and power of the Spirit. Literally, "keep on allowing yourself to be led by the Spirit." This shows that surrender is not a once-for-all matter of accessing a "second blessing" but a continual responsibility to access the blessing you received when you got saved. It is a matter of continually accessing your first blessing! It is a regular reliance upon Christ in you.

Some impulsively say, "I'll just let the Spirit take over the steering wheel of my life." But that would take your responsibility out of it, because if He was behind the wheel, you would have to go where He goes. To use this analogy, as my father often taught, the Spirit would say, "No, you stay behind the wheel. I'll stay over here in the passenger seat. Just do everything I say. Go when I say go. Stop when I say stop. Hold your tongue when I say so. Look away when I prompt you to. Turn that program off when I say so. Witness to that person when I tell you to." When you yield to His commands, you are yielding to the leadership of the Holy Spirit. In keeping with the analogy, you are the chauffeur for the Holy Spirit! You are the chauffeur for Deity!

When you are driving and someone else is navigating, if you trust your navigator, you simply follow his directions. You don't really think much about it. You just obey because you trust the one giving directions. Likewise, the Holy Spirit is a trustworthy

Navigator. Oh, that we would always trust and obey His divine navigation! The Spirit-filled life is not Spirit-control in the sense of you being an automaton. Rather it is Spirit-leadership with your cooperation.

Yield to the Spirit Regarding Sin Issues

First, always yield to the Spirit regarding sin issues. Ephesians 4:30 commands, "And grieve not the Holy Spirit of God." The grammar indicates the idea of "stop grieving the Holy Spirit." Your Heavenly Partner is a person who can be grieved. What is it that grieves the Holy Spirit? Sin! In fact the context of the last half of Ephesians 4 includes much admonition against specific sins: stealing, corrupt communication, bitterness, wrath, anger, clamor, evil speaking, and malice among others. The point is when you yield to the Spirit's leadership, all known sin must be confessed. You must deal with your sin. This does not mean sinless perfection; it means immediate confession as the Holy Spirit convicts of sin. The Spirit will not lead to media choices which please the devil. He will not lead to fashion choices which please the devil. The Holy Spirit will not lead to music choices which please the devil. Doubtful things must be done away with until you are fully convinced by the Spirit from the Scripture. Otherwise, in the name of "gray areas," you are giving Satan the benefit of the doubt, which most certainly grieves the Spirit. Reconciliation must be sought when you have wronged another and that person knows it. Restitution must be made. For example, when you yield to the Spirit, then hotel towels that are not your property must be returned!

Yield to the Spirit Regarding Self Issues

Second, always yield to the Spirit regarding self issues. I Thessalonians 5:19 commands, "Quench not the Spirit." The word *quench* simply means "to extinguish or put out as quenching fire with water." The verb is an imperative. It is a command to every child of God. This implies it is possible to quench the Spirit and thus hinder Christian growth. Therefore spiritual growth is not automatic or inevitable. Also, the grammar indicates the command is to "stop quenching the Spirit." Stop quenching the Spirit of revival! Stop dousing the flame of God's Spirit! Stop putting self over God!

In addition to obeying the negative command, positively yield to the Spirit's leadership for each step of the Christian walk. Galatians 5:16 commands, "Walk in the Spirit, and ye shall not fulfill the lust of the flesh." Verse 18 says, "But if ye be led of the Spirit, ye are not under the law." These verses imply that when you follow the leadership of the Spirit, He empowers you to overcome the law of sin. Therefore, always obey with trust; He will never lead you astray. Always say yes to His commands. Remember, the Spirit always works in harmony with the Word. I'll say more about this biblical balance of the Word and the Spirit in another chapter.

For some, "controlled carnality" is preferred to really yielding to the leadership of the Spirit. Corporately, some churches prefer tradition over true yieldedness to the Spirit as the Administrator of the church. This squelches spontaneity in corporate prayer meetings and the Spirit's liberty in public services.

You stop grieving the Spirit by dealing with sin. You stop quenching the Spirit by denying self. Thus, by keeping short accounts through immediate confession and by positively learning to trustfully obey the Spirit's voice, you are yielding to the Spirit as the Senior Partner. Yet, it is our lack of willingness on this point which holds back revival.

An evangelist from the past named R. Paul Miller tells the following story:

> During a series of meetings in Iowa, we were having hard sledding. Coldness was all around—no responses at all. After two weeks of this, on a Sunday morning the pastor, under tremendous strain, arose and slowly said, "People, I am a failure. I have worked for three years to bring about revival in this community, and I have failed. I must be a mistake in the ministry. I am resigning as pastor this morning. I don't want to stand in God's way here." The audience was astonished. They all liked him.
>
> Then a man, Mr. Williams, on the right side arose and said, "Pastor, I am not surprised that there is no revival here the way Brother Cook and I have been treating each other."
>
> They belonged to different political parties and had allowed it to enter the church. The congregation had gradually taken sides. The church was in a tragic state.
>
> Williams walked across the church to Cook's seat. Cook had an injured foot and

couldn't walk. Williams stepped up to Cook and said, "George, I'm ashamed of the things I have said about you. They were false. I'm sorry and want you to forgive me. Will you do it?"

With that, Cook stood up and said, "Howard, you're a better man than I. You came to me. I wasn't man enough to go to you. I apologize for all I have said. Forgive me."

They stood there swaying in each other's arms as the aisle filled with people streaming to the front. THEN we had revival. And what a revival! When revivals fail, someone is to blame.

You must yield to the Spirit as Lord. This gives Him His proper place as the Senior Partner. To do less is to usurp His position. Healthy partnerships recognize who is who. The Spirit is the Senior Partner; therefore you must gladly yield to His leadership. Submission is the way into blessing.

Endnotes

1. James A. Stewart, *I Must Tell* (Asheville, N.C.: Revival Literature, n. d.), pp. 86–95.

2. Ruth Stewart, *James Stewart: Missionary* (Asheville, N.C.: Revival Literature, 1977).

CHAPTER FIVE

THE EMPOWERING PARTNER

❀

Samuel Chadwick was zealous for Jesus, but God had more in store for him—the power of the Holy Spirit's fire!

Samuel Chadwick was born in the industrial north of England in 1860. His father worked long hours in the cotton mill, and when he was only eight Samuel went to work there also to help support his impoverished family.

Devout Methodists, the family attended chapel three times on Sunday, and as a young boy Chadwick gave his heart to Christ. Listening to God's Word week by week, he often felt the inner call to serve Christ. It seemed impossible, as he was poor and uneducated; but in faith he made preparations. After a twelve-hour factory shift, Chadwick would rush home for five hours of prayer and study.

At the age of 21, he was appointed lay pastor of a chapel at Stacksteads, Lancashire. It was no dream appointment; the congregation was self-satisfied. Yet Chadwick threw himself in with great optimism. He had been trained to prepare well-researched and interesting sermons as the sure way to bring in the crowds. He recalled later: "This led unconsciously to a false aim in my work. I lived and labored for my sermons, and was unfortunately more concerned about their excellence and reputation than the repentance of the people."

Soon, however, his sermons were exhausted and nothing had changed. Staring defeat in the face and sensing his lack of real power, he felt an intense hunger kindled within him for more of God. At this point he heard the testimony of someone who had been revitalized by an experience of the Holy Spirit; so with a few friends he covenanted to pray and search the Scriptures until God sent revival.

One evening as he was praying over his next sermon, a powerful sense of conviction settled on him. His pride, blindness and reliance on human methods paraded before his eyes as God humbled him to the dust. Well into the night he wrestled and repented; then he took out his pile of precious sermons and set fire to them! The result was immediate: the Holy Spirit fell upon him. In his own words: "I could not explain what had happened, but it was a bigger thing than I had ever known. There came into my soul a deep peace, a thrilling joy, and a new sense of power. My mind was quickened. I felt I had received a new faculty of understanding. Every power was vitalized. My body was quickened. There was a new sense of spring and vitality, a new power of endurance, and a strong man's exhilaration in big things."

The tide turned. After his next sermon, seven souls were converted ("one for each of my barren years"), and he called the whole congregation to a week of prayer. The following weekend most of the church was baptized in the Holy Spirit, and revival began to spread through the valleys. In the space of a few months, hundreds were converted to Jesus, among them some of the most notorious sinners in the area.[1]

Not everyone may have or need to have as dramatic an experience. But whether immediately dramatic or increasingly dramatic, everyone may and needs to know the power of the Holy Spirit. In fact, this is an absolute necessity for every believer.

Since the Spirit is the Empowering Partner, you must depend on His power. You must yield your strength to the strength of Another. You must exchange your strength, which is actually weakness, for the Spirit's strength. The Spirit-filled life is not you becoming strong, but rather you recognizing that you are weak (and always will be), and casting yourself on the Strong One. This is a life-changing realization! Simply put, you must depend on the

Spirit to live His strength through your weak, but yielded vessel. This is full surrender.

The Provision of Power

Is there really a provision of supernatural enablement for believers?

The Example of Christ

Christ was conceived of the Holy Spirit (Matthew 1:20). As believers are indwelt by the Spirit at salvation, Christ was indwelt by the Spirit at conception. Then Luke 2:40 says, "And the child grew, and waxed strong in Spirit, filled with wisdom; and the grace of God [Spirit-enablement] was upon Him." When Christ entered His three years of public ministry, He was baptized. Immediately, Luke 3:22 informs us, "the Holy Ghost descended in a bodily shape like a dove upon Him." The next event recorded in Luke 4:1 states "And Jesus being full of the Holy Ghost returned from the Jordan, and was led by the Spirit into the wilderness." There He was victorious over the devil (Luke 4:2–13). Luke 4:14–15 then states, "And Jesus returned in the power of the Spirit . . . And He taught." In the synagogue in Nazareth, Christ read from Isaiah the words "The Spirit of the Lord is upon Me, because He hath anointed Me to preach . . ." (Luke 4:18). In verse 21 He said, "This day is this Scripture fulfilled in your ears," and so on throughout His public ministry. Because He took on the limitations of a human body and set aside the use of the attributes of His own inherent Deity at His incarnation (Philippians 2:6–8), Christ did all He did in the power of the Spirit. In fact, referring to His work on the cross, Hebrews 9:14 says "who through the eternal Spirit offered Himself without spot to God."

Christ emptied Himself, not of His deity, but of the use of His divine attributes. Therefore, He had to depend on the ministry of the Holy Spirit. He set the perfect example of Spirit-dependence. If Christ in His humanity needed the ministry of the Holy Spirit, how much more do you and I!

The Promise of the Spirit

In his sermon on the Day of Pentecost, Peter stated that Christ, "being by the right hand of God exalted, and having received of the Father the promise of the Holy Ghost, He hath shed forth [lit., poured out] this, which ye now see and hear" (Acts 2:33). What is *the promise of the Holy Spirit*?

In Acts 1:4 Jesus told His disciples to "wait for the promise of the Father, which, saith He, ye have heard of Me." Forty-three days earlier in the Upper Room Discourse, Christ repeatedly promised that when He left, He and the Father would send the Spirit. How would the disciples know when this occurred? Christ explained in Acts 1:5, "Ye shall be baptized with the Holy Ghost." The definite article *the* is actually absent. Therefore Christ is grammatically emphasizing the ministry or power of the Holy Spirit. He is emphasizing "Holy Spirit-ness."

In the parallel account in Luke 24, after commissioning His disciples to be witnesses (remember at that point they were defeated men), Christ said, "And, behold, I send the promise of

My Father upon you: but tarry ye . . . until ye be endued with power from on high." In both accounts Christ urged His disciples to wait for *the promise.* In Acts, He defined this as being *baptized with* [the power of] *the Holy Spirit.* In Luke, He defined this as being *endued with power from on high.* Therefore the promise of the Spirit is a promise of power!

Positionally, this occurs at salvation. Galatians 3:26–27 says, "For ye are all the children of God by faith in Christ Jesus. For as many of you as have been baptized into Christ have put on Christ." *Have put on* comes from the word translated in Luke 24:49 *be endued.* We already noted that in Acts 1:5 *be endued* is parallel with *be baptized.* So when you believed in Christ, not only were you baptized into Christ when the Spirit placed you into Christ, you were also baptized or endued with Christ when Christ placed His Spirit into you. This is a fact for every believer.

However, experientially this must be accessed by faith. Galatians 3:14 explains that we are justified "that we might receive the promise of the Spirit *through faith.*" Although we are given the indwelling Spirit at salvation, we must take by faith His power. The phrase *that we might receive* shows that this is a responsibility, not an inevitability. *Through faith* makes it abundantly clear that faith turns the positional facts into experiential function. We'll say more about this access of faith in a moment. However, first let's note the commands regarding this responsibility.

The Necessity of Power

Not only is the power of the Spirit a necessity because of our need seen through the example of Christ and the promised power to meet our need, but also because Scripture commands us to avail ourselves of this blessed power.

Be Filled with the Spirit

When Ephesians 5:18 commands, "Be filled with the Spirit," the definite article *the* is actually absent, indicating an emphasis on the power or operation of the person. Not only are we to yield to the Spirit's leadership, we must also depend on the Spirit's enablement to follow that leadership. The Spirit not only gives us orders, but when depended upon, He empowers us to carry out those very orders! Again II Corinthians 3:17 says, "Where the Spirit of the Lord is [or where the Spirit is Lord], there is liberty." Not just the right to do right, but the liberty to do right. This is true Christian liberty. Not the freedom to do as you please, but the freedom or power to do right. This is liberty indeed!

Spirit-enablement accessed by faith liberates the personality for God's service and glory. No longer is the personality animated by mere human life, but rather by divine life. This gives carrying power to a formerly powerless child of God. This is the revived life. The confusion comes on the extent of surrender. Some sincere souls cry out, "I surrender all, and I'm going to do it!" The problem is that you cannot live for God in your power. It is not His will, your way. If you surrender to the Spirit's leadership, but then depend on your power to attempt to carry it out, you really have not surrendered to His leadership. This leaves the "surrender" empty and powerless, and the believer is left perplexed and discouraged. True surrender depends on the Spirit's leadership *and* His enablement to follow His leadership.

Just as one does not believe in Jesus until he depends on Jesus as Savior, so you really do not believe in the Holy Spirit until you are depending on the Holy Spirit for everything. It is then that the Spirit of Christ gives you experientially the sufficiency of Christ, which you already possess positionally as a child of God. Surrender and faith are the access. This is not a second blessing. This is accessing your first blessing.

Some misunderstand the Spirit-filled life to be only Spirit-leadership, and they miss the truth that the Spirit-filled life is also Spirit-empowerment. If the Spirit-filled life is just Spirit-leadership, then "just obey" is the key. But obedience through flesh-dependence profits nothing (John 6:63). Or if the Spirit-filled life is only Spirit-empowerment, then "just trust" is the key. But trusting for what you want is not the same as trusting for what God wants. However, if the Spirit-filled life is a matter of Spirit-leadership and Spirit-empowerment, then "trust to obey" is the key. Certainly, you must yield to the Spirit's leadership, but you also must depend on His power to enable you to follow His leading. No one can "just obey" the Word of God without the power of God. God-dependence accesses Spirit-enablement.

You and I cannot live the Spirit-filled life in our own power. The Spirit-filled life is a Life—a Person—living through your yielded, dependent vessel. The Spirit-filled life, the victorious life, the deeper life, the higher life is not a new line of teaching, a mere set of doctrines, a mere set of moral motions, a conference, or a movement; it is a Life—and His name is Jesus! The Spirit of Jesus moved into you to live His life, not yours! As long as you live your life, you will veil His life. But when you stop living your life, He will manifest His life. No one can live the Christian life but Christ—and He lives in you! So that you can live (yet not you, but Christ in you) the Christian life.

Walk in the Spirit

The command of Galatians 5:16 to "walk in the Spirit" reveals that this reality is not automatic. We are commanded to *walk*, not simply sit back and assume we are Spirit-filled. But what does it mean to walk in the Spirit?

Colossians 2:6 explains, "As ye have therefore received Christ Jesus the Lord, so walk ye in him." How did you receive Christ? By surrendering to the conviction of the Holy Spirit regarding sin, righteousness, and judgment and choosing to depend on Christ to save you. So how do you *walk in Him*? How do you *walk in the Spirit*? By surrendering to the Spirit's leadership for the next step and choosing to depend on His power to take that step.

Walking is reiterated steps. Therefore, walking in the Spirit is reiterated steps in the Spirit. This reveals that partnership with the Spirit is simply one step at a time. You need not look backward or fear the future. Satan may urge you to look backward, perhaps to discourage you with the thought that you are "too bad" to ever be used of God. Or he may urge you to fear the future with the thought that it is only a matter of time and you will "blow it." Either focus can move you from the position of faith. But if you are presently trusting, then He is presently enabling.

This is not a matter of "just obey," for unsaved moralists can go through the motions. Nor is it a matter of "just trust," which is no trust at all but passivity. It is a matter of "trust to obey." God-dependence accesses Spirit-enablement as the power to actually obey. What a blessing—there is hope! Just as when Jesus told the paralyzed man to take up his bed and walk (which was humanly impossible), so when the Spirit of Jesus commands you to think rightly, speak the soft answer, or declare the gospel, it may seem impossible. But just as the paralyzed man received miraculous strength when he, by faith, reached for the bed, so when you depend on the Spirit for that impossible step, He supernaturally enables you to actually take the step. Victory in Christ is victory without trying. But victory without trying is not victory doing nothing; it is victory with trusting! That demands the step of faith. This is not idle passivity; it is active cooperation.

One dear lady wrote to me to testify of this reality in the matter of the gospel. She had never led a soul to Christ. But she determined to obey the Spirit and depend on His power. When the Spirit prompted her to witness to an unsaved teen girl, she said she was terrified. Thankfully, faith is not a feeling, and when she took the step of faith by opening her mouth, she said it was as if the Holy Spirit just took over. By the second conversation the next day, the girl made a decision to trust Christ as her Savior!

How much would change if we lived the life of surrender and faith! What blessings we would receive, what victory in Christ we would access, and what joy we would know! Since the Holy Spirit is the Empowering Partner, we must depend on His power. But how do we depend on His power?

The Access of Power

The access revolves around three simple words: *ask, take, act.*

Ask

Luke 11:13 is so simple and so clear: "If ye then, being evil, know how to give good gifts unto your children; how much more shall your heavenly Father give the Holy Spirit to them that **ask** Him?" Some may object, saying that this is no longer valid because it was given before the Day of Pentecost. But keep in mind, Luke inscribed this promise under inspiration long after the Day of Pentecost. Would this glorious promise be inscribed under the inspiration of the Holy Spirit when it was no longer valid? Obviously not. This promise is for today!

How much more indicates the Father delights in granting this request. The definite article *the* is absent before the name Holy Spirit, indicating the ministry, operation, or power of the Spirit—*Holy Spirit-ness.*

We are to ask for the power of the Holy Spirit. Also *ask* is in the present tense, indicating continuous action. In other words, this is not a one-time event, but a repeated event. We find this illustrated throughout the Book of Acts. In Acts 1:14, they prayed. In Acts 2:4, they were "filled with the Holy Ghost." In Acts 4, they prayed again, and again they "were all filled with the Holy Ghost, and they spake the word of God with boldness." And so on throughout the Book of Acts.

Jesus said *ask*, just simply *ask*! Regardless of your level of understanding, just ask for the power of the Holy Spirit. God will straighten out in you what needs to be adjusted so that He can answer, for *how much more shall your heavenly Father give [the power of] the Holy Spirit to them that ask Him.*

Take

Acts 1:8 says "But ye shall receive power, after that the Holy Ghost is come upon you." Here the future tense is used as an imperative much like a parent saying "you will do this!" *Receive* is often translated "take." Notice it does not say "ye shall be given power," but rather *ye shall receive power.* You are responsible to take by faith what you are asking for. The next phrase in Acts 1:8 is difficult to trans-late. Actually, there is no preposition. Awkwardly, but literally, it says "the Holy Spirit coming on you." So ask in faith for the power of the Spirit, and then take by faith the power of the Spirit regardless of your feelings.

When my son asks me for a piece of candy, and I hold a piece out to him, he always takes it! Likewise, simply ask for the Spirit's power and simply take it by faith.

Act

Acts 1:8 then commands "and ye shall be witnesses unto Me." Ask, take, and then in faith act upon the reality that the Spirit is enabling you. Here the step of obedience is witnessing. As you open your mouth to witness, the Spirit will enable you for the step of obedience you are taking. This is trusting to obey. This is partnership with the Spirit of power!

When David O'Gorman, whom I mentioned in Chapter One, was a fairly new believer studying for the ministry, he was stirred with the promise of Luke 11:13. Early in his ministry, he preached the simple truth of the verse. But at that time an older preacher told him that Luke 11:13 was not for today. As a young preacher, David's faith was undermined. This led to sincere but frustrated ministry. During the revival mentioned in Chapter One, God brought him back to faith regarding the promise of Luke 11:13. Since then the difference that trusting for divine unction has made in his life and ministry is like the difference between night and day.

The same will be true for you. Simply ask, take, and act. As you do, God will manifest His reality through the surrendered, dependent channel of your life!

Endnotes

1. Samuel Chadwick, *The Way to Pentecost* (Great Britain: Hodder and Stouten Ltd., 1932; reprint ed., Fort Washington, Pa.: Christian Literature Crusade Publications, 2001), pp. 7–9.

CHAPTER SIX

A SACRED TRUST

⚛

Downtown Chicago is a favorite spot my wife and I like to visit. One winter we walked down Michigan Avenue. For the fun of it, I suggested we go into one of the fancy stores. When I saw long fur coats, not only on the mannequins but also on the customers, I realized that we were in the wrong place! In stores such as this, several things are observable in the jewelry section. Valuable jewels remain encased under lock and key. Small cameras keep a watchful eye on browsing customers. Also, a man in uniform, armed with a gun, makes his presence known. Clearly stores such as this are guarding something that they consider to be valuable. In like manner, you must guard your friendship with the Holy Spirit, which is more valuable than any jewel.

Acts 2:33 declares that Jesus, "being by the right hand of God exalted, and having received of the Father the promise of the Holy Ghost, He hath shed forth [poured out] this, which ye now see and hear." On the Day of Pentecost, Christ sent the Spirit, and the Spirit has not been sent back. This reality allows for the truth of II Corinthians 13:14 to take place. There can actually be *communion* with the Holy Spirit. Since you live in the dispensation of the Spirit, you must guard your friendship with the Holy Spirit. How does this unfold, what are the consequences, and what is the key protection?

The Dispensations of the Godhead

When reading true classics on the Holy Spirit, one will most certainly be blessed in reading J. Elder Cumming's *Through the Eternal Spirit,* Handley Moule's *The Holy Spirit,* and A. J. Gordon's *The Ministry of the Spirit.* Later writers often quote from these works. All three emanate with reverence and biblical precision on the subject of the Holy Spirit. Both Moule and Gordon refer to a concept we might term "the dispensations of the Godhead." These divine dispensations dictate as it were some divine tests of living orthodoxy. Satan's attack on God's people then parallels the emphasis of each dispensation. Note the following distinctions.

The Dispensation of the Father

The Old Testament could be termed "the dispensation of the Father." The person of God the Father clearly is in prominence. The emphasis is on the oneness of God. Therefore the test of living orthodoxy for the people of God during that dispensation was regarding that emphasis. Consequently, Satan's attack was on that very point. Do we not read repeatedly of Israel's great sin of idolatry?

The Dispensation of the Son

Christ's coming to earth at the first advent might be termed "the dispensation of the Son." (It will not be the only one.) As you read the Gospels, clearly God the Son is seen in prominence. The test of living orthodoxy for the people of God revolved around Jesus Christ. Would those who were orthodox regarding the Father now properly receive and relate to the Son? Therefore, Satan's attack on God's people shifted to the Son. What does the Scripture say? "He came unto His own, and His own received Him not" (John 1:11).

The Dispensation of the Holy Spirit

Christ finished His glorious work at Calvary and ascended to the right hand of the throne of power. There He received the promise of the Spirit and sent the Holy Spirit. This event launched what may be termed "the dispensation of God the Spirit," and the Holy Spirit has not been sent back yet. Therefore, we now live in the age of the Holy Spirit. The Spirit is the Administrator of the church age. The test of living orthodoxy today for God's people regards the Holy Spirit. Will those who are orthodox regarding the Father and the Son now properly receive and relate to the Spirit? Therefore, Satan's attack on God's people has shifted to this very point.

In Revelation 2–3 in the messages sent to the churches of this age, the Scripture repeatedly says, "He that hath an ear, let him hear what the Spirit saith unto the churches." Notice the emphasis on *the Spirit*. At the beginning of the dispensation of the Spirit, is it not significant that when Ananias sinned, Peter said, "Why hath Satan filled thine heart to lie to the Holy Ghost?" (Acts 5:3). Notice Satan's attack and notice that the lie was directly against the Holy Spirit. Why did Peter not say the Father or the Son? Because this is the age or dispensation of the Spirit and inspiration here clearly portrays this very point.

The Present Attack: Strange Fire and No Fire

Need I say that over these past 2,000 years Satan has persisted with this attack? Although the attack among the lost revolves around all three persons of the Godhead, the attack among the saints pertains primarily to the Holy Spirit. In light of what we have just noted, this should not surprise us.

Consequently, many refer to the Holy Spirit as "it." Many attempt service for Christ without seeking the leadership of the Spirit and/or without depending on Him for effective service. Some focus on the gifts of the Spirit instead of the God of the gifts. Some embrace counterfeits of the Spirit. Satan has done all he can to keep the saints from a right understanding and relationship to the Holy Spirit.

James A. Stewart, a missionary evangelist from Scotland who saw revival repeatedly during his itinerate lifetime, wrote a book on the ministry of the Holy Spirit entitled *Heaven's Throne Gift*. Keep in mind he wrote this book before the Charismatic movement of the 1960s. In the book he points out that you could take a group of fundamental preachers, and they would all agree regarding God the Father and regarding God the Son. But he continues that they would disagree regarding God the Spirit and that the disagreement would be so sharp that fellowship would be strained and some would accuse others of false doctrine.[1]

Then the 1960s brought the Charismatic explosion, which took elements of Pentecostal thinking beyond denominational lines. Although there were and are many sincere brethren within this movement, biblical fundamentalists and conservative evangelicals rightly rejected the excesses of the Charismatic movement. Truly there are excesses which reveal the mark of satanic deception or show the marks of fleshly imitation. The resulting dual streams of power weaken or discredit real fire. However, I fear that in the understandable and needed reaction against strange fire, there has been an overreaction which embraces no fire! Orthodoxy without the life of the Spirit is dead orthodoxy. Satan knows that a believer who is not rightly related to the Holy Spirit is powerless.

Some today, in their desire to put out strange fire, have de-emphasized biblical subjectivism, which is the real, interactive ministry of the Holy Spirit based on biblical truth. This leads to sheer objectivism. My preacher-father used to say, "Pure objectivism is one step away from liberalism." Liberalism denies the supernatural, while pure objectivism minimizes the supernatural. Therefore, it is one step away from liberalism. On the other hand, pure subjectivism is also one step away from liberalism. Liberalism denies the inerrant, divine revelation, while pure subjectivism minimizes it. Therefore, it is also one step away. The key is the Word (objective truth) and the Spirit (subjective truth based on objective truth). Jesus said that we must "worship Him [God] in spirit and in truth" (John 4:24).

The Spirit without the Word is delusion. The Word without the Spirit is deadness. But the combination of the Word and the Spirit is dynamic! Some today minimize any specific leading of the Spirit and simply point to the Word. However, this ignores the reality of *communion* with the Spirit. Also, this thinking practically denies the personality of the Spirit. While strange fire (in the name of the Spirit) must be rejected, no fire (in the name of the Word) is not the answer. The key is the Word *and* the Spirit. The Spirit always works in harmony with the Word. The legitimate subjective realm is according to the objective boundaries of the Word. Therefore, on the one hand you must not allow deadness to lead you to delusion, and on the other hand you must not allow strange fire to lead you to no fire.

The Holy Spirit does specifically lead and empower. Jesus taught in Luke 12:11-12, "And when they bring you unto the synagogues, and unto magistrates, and powers, take ye no thought how or what thing ye shall answer, or what ye shall say: For the Holy Ghost shall teach you in the same hour what ye ought to say." Jesus taught the specific leading of the Spirit. Acts 8, 10, 13, and 16 all illustrate the Spirit's specific leading. Romans 8:14 speaks of being "led by the Spirit." Galatians 5:18 speaks of being "led of the Spirit." As the "Spirit of wisdom" in Ephesians 1:17, obviously the Spirit gives wisdom. Truly there is a specific leading of the Spirit based on biblical truth. Just because some may follow their own whims or a satanic counterfeit does not mean there is not a real leading of the Holy Spirit. How can you "try the spirits" according to I John 4:1 if there is no genuine leading of the Spirit? Ironically, if Satan can prompt as he did in Acts 5 with Ananias, certainly the Holy Spirit can prompt!

Some note the parallel between Ephesians 5:18–19, "Be filled with the Spirit; Speaking to yourselves in psalms and hymns and spiritual songs, singing and making melody in your heart to the Lord," and Colossians 3:16, "Let the word of Christ dwell in you richly in all wisdom; teaching and admonishing one another in psalms and hymns and spiritual songs, singing with grace in your hearts to the Lord." They then argue that the real issue is the Word, not the Spirit. But this same kind of logic could argue that the real issue is the Spirit, not the Word. Is it not obvious the Bible emphasizes the Word *and* the Spirit?

Every Spirit-filled believer must of necessity be Word-filled. For you cannot access the Spirit but by faith, which has the Word as its foundation. Some may learn the Word merely on the intellectual level, but they do not depend on it. Without faith therefore, they are not Spirit-filled. But every Spirit-filled believer must of necessity be Word-filled. Some argue that you do not need to surrender to the Spirit; you just need to surrender to the Word. But who authored the Word through the biblical writers, and who illumines and convinces you of the Word? The Spirit. Cannot we see the importance of both? II

Corinthians 3:6 explains "For the letter killeth, but the Spirit giveth life." The issue is not the Word or the Spirit, but the Word and the Spirit.

In all of this we can note a subtle apostasy within conservative Christianity. Full-blown apostasy in doctrine often begins with an apostasy in practice. On the one hand, in de-emphasizing the Holy Spirit, some have unwittingly begun a subtle apostasy in practice (no experience). On the other hand, some who have recognized deadness and powerlessness have sadly embraced a counterfeit life. When worldliness and carnal conduct is ignored or even embraced as a marketing tool, there has also been an apostasy in practice (false experience). Eventually apostasy in doctrine often follows. In both cases, where does the apostasy (falling away) begin? It begins with a falling away from a right relationship with the Holy Spirit. This is the cause for powerlessness and worldliness. This subtle apostasy from the Holy Spirit's person and power leads to apostasy in practice that leads to apostasy in doctrine.

Furthermore, as Moule (quoting John Owen) acknowledges in his book, neglecting the ministry of the Holy Spirit today is on the same level as Israel's idolatry in the Old Testament and the Jews' rejection of the Messiah.[2] To slight the Holy Spirit today is to slight Christ's throne gift for this age. The sent Spirit of the glorified Christ is the gift of the Spirit from Christ for this dispensation. Is it not alarming that sound, fundamental people today have played right into Satan's deceptive tactics? In running from the wild fire of others, some have stumbled right into the trap of subtle apostasy from the Holy Spirit by de-emphasizing the Spirit. Yet it is the Spirit who indwells believers to enable those who trust Him to do the work of God. As A. W. Tozer said, "The Holy Spirit is the cure for fanaticism, not the cause of it."

Others, in repulsion to the dead form of godliness that denies the power thereof, have embraced a counterfeit sense of life. Yet the Holy Spirit leads to holiness, not worldliness. When either the Holy Spirit or holiness is de-emphasized, the result is a flesh-filled life. Some Charismatics have ignored holiness (separation from the world), and therefore indulge in the works of the flesh. Some biblical fundamentalists have ignored the Holy Spirit, and therefore depend on the strength of the flesh. Both are flesh-filled. The answer is a right relationship with the Spirit of holiness.

The Key Protection: The Word of God

The major protection to guard your relationship with the Holy Spirit from strange fire is the Word of God. The Spirit without the Word is not the Spirit—it is delusion. This is what leads to strange fire. "The Spirit of truth" (John 14:17; 15:26; 16:13) will always work according to the Word of truth (John 17:17). The Spirit as the author of Scripture (II Peter 1:21) will not violate Himself. Therefore, Holy Spirit leadership is always in harmony with the principles of God's Word. The Spirit never speaks contrary to the Word. The Spirit will never lead you to do wrong in order to get a chance to do right. Also, it is dangerous to trust impressions alone, for Satan is a good deceiver. Biblical principle (truth) is the key to discerning satanic counterfeits.[3]

For example, the Word of God explains how the Spirit of God guides. Galatians 5:18 speaks of being "led by the Spirit." Counterfeit guidance drives or pushes, and does not allow time to "try the spirits whether they are of God" (1 John 4:1). 1 Corinthians 14:33 says, "God is not the author of confusion, but of peace." Counterfeit guidance prompts in a "zigzag" fashion which irritates and eliminates peace by causing one to leave the position of resting in Christ. Romans 8:16 says, "The Spirit ... bears witness with our spirit." The Spirit communicates within your inner man. This is a knowledge versus a feeling. Counterfeit guidance is from your circumference or outer man or even outside voices and so forth. Ephesians 4:23 refers to "the Spirit of your mind" letting us know that the Spirit works through your mind, not around it. Counterfeit guidance bypasses the normal function of the thinking process.

Another example is in the realm of conviction. Holy Spirit conviction is specific and has as its goal cleansing and victory in Christ (1 John 16:11; 1 John 1:7, 9; John 16:14). Counterfeit conviction is general and has as its goal discouragement and despair by accusing the brethren (Revelation 12:10). These examples demonstrate how the objective realm of the Word provides the parameters in which the subjective realm of the Spirit operates.

Lack of grounding in the Word regarding the Holy Spirit allows Satan to quickly counterfeit real fire and quench real revival. Those who embrace counterfeits may be sincere and even surrendered to the supernatural realm. But if they do not discern between the Holy Spirit and evil spirits, they can be grossly deceived. Imitation is also counterfeit and must be rejected based on the revealed Word of truth. However, real fire must be accepted based on that same Word of truth. It is the Word which instructs us in the legitimate and needful realm of the Holy Spirit. The Word of God is the key protection against both strange fire and no fire.

For many, their partnership with the Spirit is a dysfunctional partnership. Much of this occurs because of a lack of heeding Christ's own teaching—His Word—regarding His Spirit. In John 14:7, Jesus says, "If ye had known Me, ye should have known My Father also: and from henceforth ye know Him, and have seen Him." Notice that the phrase *ye know Him* indicates that the disciples knew the Father because they knew the Son. A few verses later in John 14:16–17, Jesus says, "And I will pray the Father, and He shall give you another Comforter, that He may abide with you forever; Even the Spirit of truth; whom the world cannot receive, because it seeth Him not, neither knoweth Him: but ye know Him; for He dwelleth with you, and shall be in you." Notice Jesus again uses the phrase *ye know Him,* this time referring to the Spirit. When Christ then emphasizes that the Spirit *shall be in you*, He explains in the next verse, "I will not leave you comfortless: I will come to you." The Spirit in you is Christ in you! Therefore to ignore, neglect, slight, or despise the Holy Spirit today, even if well intentioned, is actually ignoring, neglecting, slighting, or despising Christ. Oh, that God's people would wake up to the blessed coming of Christ to them through the Holy Spirit!

No wonder Jesus said in John 16:7, "It is expedient for you [to your advantage] that I go away: for if I go not away, the Comforter will not come unto you; but if I depart, I will send Him unto you." When Christ walked on earth, He could be in only one place at a time because of the limitations of His human body; but by ascending and sending His Spirit, He could now be personally with each disciple everywhere at all times. Not only would the Spirit of Christ dwell *with* each disciple, He would dwell *in* each disciple! What a blessed plan of God that Deity would be incorporated into human personality! This is friendship with the Holy Spirit.

Friendship with the Spirit is not your struggling, not your trying, but rather your trusting Christ in you to express His life through your weak, but surrendered, dependent channel. When this reality of Galatians 2:20 was brought home to me, what a difference this partnership began to make in my own personal pilgrimage. "I live; yet not I, but Christ liveth in me." Will you guard your friendship with the Holy Spirit? Without that vibrant partnership, you are powerless and ineffective in the cause of Christ.

Endnotes

1. James A. Stewart, *Heaven's Throne Gift* (Asheville, N.C.: Revival Literature, 1956, 2001), p. 66.
2. Handley G. C. Moule, *The Holy Spirit* (1890; reprint ed., Great Britain: Christian Focus Publications, 1999), p. 8.
3. For a thorough treatise on discerning satanic counterfeits in the spirit realm, see *War on the Saints* by Jessie Penn-Lewis with Evan Roberts, published by Lowe. Some of the major principles which I have learned from *War on the Saints* are in Appendixes B, C, and D in my book *The Wind of the Spirit in Personal and Corporate Revival,* published by Preach the Word Ministries, Inc.

CHAPTER SEVEN

The Revival Relationship

⚜

*T*he grace of the Lord Jesus Christ, and the love of God, and the communion of the Holy Ghost be with you all. Amen* (II Corinthians 13:14). Communion with the Holy Spirit—is this real in your life? What is the Holy Spirit to you? What does the Spirit mean to you? How is your relationship with the Holy Spirit? Do you have a vibrant friendship with the Spirit? We began our study with these questions. Since then, we have been investigating what it means to live in partnership with the Holy Spirit.

Since you are to commune with the Holy Spirit, you must develop a friendship with your Heavenly Partner. In order for you, as the human partner, to properly relate with the Spirit as the Heavenly Partner, you must know who He is to you. We've seen that the Spirit is the Divine Partner. As such, you must honor Him as God. We've seen that He is a Personal Partner. As such, you must treat Him as a person. We've noted that the Spirit is clearly the Senior Partner. As such, you must yield to Him as

Lord. We've seen that the Spirit is the Empowering Partner. As such, you must depend on Him for enablement. We've also investigated the dispensation of the Spirit in which we live right now. Therefore, you must guard your relationship with the Spirit from Satan's insidious attack.

When you know the Spirit as God, treat the Spirit as a person, yield to the Spirit as Lord by surrendering to His leadership and depending on His enablement, and carefully guard this friendship, you have entered into the revival relationship. *Revive* means "life again." *Re* (again) + *vive* (life) is a restoration to life. To be revived physically is to be restored to physical life. To be revived spiritually is to be restored to spiritual life—life in the Spirit! Revival, whether personal or corporate, always restores individuals to a right relationship with the Holy Spirit. This is friendship with the Spirit. It is the Spirit-filled life for holiness and service. Will you live in the reality of your partnership with the Spirit through surrender and faith?

Let's finish the story we began with Walter Wilson back at the end of Chapter One. Remember, through the kind confrontation of a man of God, Wilson had become desirous "to know the Spirit and to serve Him successfully." From his book on the Spirit, *Ye Know Him*, he relates the following:

About this time the Lord very graciously sent a devoted minister from Chicago who brought a wonderful message on Romans 12:1. Having finished his address on the subject, he leaned over the pulpit and said, "It is the Holy Spirit to whom you are to give your body. Your body is the temple of the Holy Spirit, and you are requested in this passage to give it to Him for His possession. Will you do this tonight?"

I left the service deeply impressed with the thought that no doubt here was the answer to my deep need and the relief from my barren life. Upon arriving home I went to my study and laid myself flat on the carpet with my Bible open at Romans 12:1. Placing my finger on the passage, I said to the Holy Spirit, "Never before have I come to you with myself: I do so now. You may have my body, my lips, my feet, my brain, my hands, and all that I am and have. My body is yours for you to live within and do as you please. Just now I make you my Lord and I receive you as my own personal God. I shall see your wonderful working in my life, and I know you will make Christ very real to my heart. I thank you for accepting me for you said the gift is 'acceptable.' I thank you for this gracious meeting with yourself tonight."

Upon rising the next morning I said to my wife, "This will be a wonderful day. Last evening I received the Holy Spirit into my life as my Lord and gave Him my body to use for His glory and for the honor of the Lord Jesus. I know He will do it and He will use me without a doubt." She replied, "If anything unusual happens today, call me on the phone. I will be anxious to know." About eleven o'clock I had the joy of phoning home that the Spirit had spoken through my lips to the hearts of two young women, sisters, who had entered my office on business. Both of them trusted the Savior. This was the beginning of new days of victory, blessing, and fruitfulness which have continued since that time. I ceased to neglect and ignore this gracious Person who had come to live with me. Now He was free to use me in His service for the glory of the Lord Jesus.

Your days, too, will be transformed and your life made fruitful if you will give to the Holy Spirit the place He should have in your life.[1]

Friendship with the Spirit is the revival relationship. Will you enter into the reality of your privileged partnership? This is the need of the hour individually and corporately.

Pastor Ron Vanderhart told me, soon after we arrived on a Saturday in August of 2003, that perhaps fifteen people in his congregation had "burning hearts." He said, "God is doing something!" About a year or so earlier, the church had been going through some severe trials. At that time, Pastor Vanderhart's son Scott, who was also assistant pastor of the church, read A. W. Tozer's book *The Pursuit of God*. A spark was ignited! As the pastor and others read the book too, soon there was a "fellowship of burning hearts."

They began to meet on Saturday mornings and desperately cry out to God for revival.

One year later, we arrived for a weeklong meeting. When I heard of those with burning hearts, I began to sense that God really was doing something. Interestingly, the Spirit had moved me just a few days before this to begin praying for an outpouring of the Spirit—now! The Spirit continued to enable me to pray this way.

By Sunday evening, I was aware of some of the burning hearts. By Tuesday, the truths of a clean heart and the reality of the Spirit-filled life began to take hold in some lives. On Wednesday evening I preached on "Partnership with the Holy Spirit." After a precious service in which many responded to truth, I announced that those who were able and so desired could reconvene in fifteen minutes. I'll let excerpts from my journal tell the story:

> I publicly turned the meeting over to the Holy Spirit, encouraging each one to pray, sing, or testify only as the Spirit guided. After opening in prayer, the pastor prayed a sweet confession regarding neglecting the Holy Spirit. He was manifestly moved. Soon, his sons prayed honest, transparent, earnest prayers.... There followed confession after confession with a broken spirit. Songs interspersed the praying. After a time of real cleansing, there was prayer for lost loved ones. One man prayed with real brokenness regarding the state of his children. Another lady wept and prayed over

her grandchildren. Truly, God had manifested His presence! The meeting lasted for one hour and forty-five minutes.

Thursday . . . we met again for an after-meeting. The first 20–30 minutes seemed hard. Several even mentioned it in their prayers. I sensed an attack from the evil one. So I explained the basics of spiritual warfare. I urged that each one ask God to search them and deal with any sin God brought to light, but that if nothing came to light, recognize a direct attack from the powers of darkness and to plead the blood and promises of Christ's victory over Satan at the cross. The Lord led me to then pray accordingly. Then He prompted me to lead in singing "There Is Power in the Blood." . . . The next hour was one of the most glorious hours I, perhaps, have ever witnessed. "Where the Spirit of the Lord is; there is liberty." O what liberty! It was an hour of some of the sweetest, deepest, most earnest confessions and honesty before the Lord who knows all. God had come down. Also, there was both soul searching and glorious singing. Again, the praying turned toward a passion for the lost. The meeting lasted for over two hours and ended sometime after 11:00 P.M. On Friday . . . we definitely had increased in those who came. Again God met with us for over two hours! Many confessed failure in the Gospel. We finished again around 11:00 P.M.

Nine months later, the assistant pastor, Scott, told me, "There is no question. A group of people have been definitely changed!" Hallelujah! This was God-sent revival. Nearly every time I have spoken with Pastor Vanderhart, he says that the effects of the revival still continue. Friendship with the Spirit is real!

The following week, after the revival, a few of these folks came to my next meeting. I asked several to give a testimony. Scott testified that ten minutes of prayer used to seem like two hours; but that now, two hours in prayer seem like ten minutes! He also said, "If you would have asked me a week ago what revival was, I could not have told you." Then, as a tear rolled down his cheek, he said, "Now I can tell you what revival is—it's Jesus Christ!"

Oh that we would realize the Spirit glorifies the Son! If you partner with the Spirit, Christ will be glorified. When you develop a vibrant friendship with the Spirit, you will be aglow with the indwelling Christ! No wonder the inspired prayer of Paul was *the communion of the Holy Ghost be with you all. Amen.*

Endnotes

1. Walter Wilson, *Ye Know Him* (Grand Rapids: Zondervan, 1939), pp. 10–11.

RECOMMENDED READING

꙳

Cumming, J. Elder. *Through the Eternal Spirit*. Minneapolis: Bethany Fellowship, Inc., 1965.

Gordan, A. J. *The Ministry of the Spirit*. Minneapolis: Bethany House Publishers, reprint 1985.

Moule, Handley G. C. *The Holy Spirit*. Great Britain: Christian Focus Publications, 1890, reprint 1999.

Murray, Andrew. *The Spirit of Christ*. Minneapolis: Bethany House Publishers, reprint 1979.

Stewart, James A. *Heaven's Throne Gift*. Asheville, N.C.: Revival Literature, 1956, reprint 2001.

Torrey, R. A. *The Person and Work of the Holy Spirit*. New Kensington, Pa.: Whitaker House, reprint 1996.

Wilson, Walter. *Ye Know Him*. Grand Rapids: Zondervan, 1939.

Printed in the United States
140231LV00001B/14/A

9 781600 348624